The Dustbowl

Also by Jim Goar

Seoul Bus Poems
The Louisiana Purchase

Jim Goar

The Dustbowl

Shearsman Books

First published in the United Kingdom in 2014 by
Shearsman Books
50 Westons Hill Drive
Emersons Green
BRISTOL
BS16 7DF

Shearsman Books Ltd Registered Office
30-31 St. James Place, Mangotsfield, Bristol BS16 9JB
(this address not for correspondence)

www.shearsman.com

ISBN 978-1-84861-321-8

Copyright © Jim Goar, 2014.
The right of Jim Goar to be identified as the author
of this work has been asserted by him in accordance with the
Copyrights, Designs and Patents Act of 1988.
All rights reserved.

Acknowledgements

Pieces from *The Dustbowl* were published in *Blackbox Manifold, Dusie, English, The Hardy Review, Jacket Magazine, New Writing, Parameter, Poetry Wales, Raleigh Quarterly*, and the anthology *Dear World & Everyone In It: new poetry in the UK*. Thank you to the editors. I'd also like to thank Tony Frazer, Marcus Slease, Jeremy Noel-Tod, George Szirtes, and the good people in the Rose and York Taverns for helping make Norwich home.

For Sang-yeon

Notes from the Dustbowl

	Page No		Page No
#10	9	#62	37
#11	10	#64	38
#20	11	#65	39
#21	12	#67	40
#24	13	#68	41
#30	14	#69	42
#32	15	#70	43
#34	16	#71	44
#35	17	#72	45
#36	18	#73	46
#37	19	#74	47
#38	20	#75	48
#39	21	#76	49
#41	22	#77	50
#42	23	#78	51
#43	24	#79	52
#46	25	#80	53
#48	26	#81	54
#49	27	#82	55
#50	28	#83	56
#51	29	#84	57
#52	30	#85	58
#54	31	#86	59
#55	32	#87	60
#56	33	#88	61
#57	34	#89	62
#58	35	#91	63
#59	36		

The '#' denotes the order of composition. The first poem of *The Dustbowl* was the tenth composed. These poems remain in the order written, though some poems have been discarded, including those beyond #91.

The Dustbowl

Ghost town. Tumbleweed. Ain't got no home. Ain't got no home. But an echo. A stutter. The land like magic shit. Behold the dustbowl. That Damn-ward sun. Big as your fist. Sit on Plymouth Rock. I'll sit below. Contemplating West. Forget-me-not.

The slaughter of prophecy. Didn't see
that coming. All my doves and not a single
returned. The plan was simple. Forget
the forest loomed. Blackbirds at
my ear. Conversation. Bird language.
No paper trail. My Grandfather in a
nest. Didn't ask the question. Not
eggs of plenty. Each memory a wife.
Yoke me she said. Yoke her I did.
I don't work there anymore.

When the wind blows
night. And the cows roll
home. Listen for minor
keys. Arrive without a
name. A Texas Ranger.
Maybe. The Grail in tow.
Ride on out of town. Leave.
But slowly. April in the waste-
land. In No-Man's-Land. In snow.

Let me recap: At the time
there were no bad guys.
Wrote myself into a corner.
Needed a Christmas Dinner. A
knight more pure than green.
A noble calling. Pulled Galahad
from the lake. Intended to
sleep under his wet blanket. And
then another. Stole your life
preserver. Pirates on the Florida
coast. Not worthy of the Grail.

I am a radio short and stout. Didn't want to spoil the end. Returned to a red and black dragon. Knew the priest was your father. Way down in a hole. No chance. Always rolling loaded dice. A different game. Told what I could. Grails on the outfield fence. Blooming cloud of good. See? Exported cricket with Arthur. Now yours. Keep them well. A little boy fell in a well. An evil sister closing in.

Kept a false Grail amongst her
knightly things. Drank from
that cold winter cup. Knew
the red coats were waiting.
One Mississippi. Two miss-
issippi. A flood of bad English.
No-man's-land in sight. The ocean
under-stood. A fish out of water.
Knock-knock. Who's there?
Poor Galahad on Mars.

Pinned the Grail to my chest. Promissed a return. Rode into the desert. Never saw me again. Became the wild frontier. Bore dustbowls. Made depressions. Lived in your heartlands. Imagined heaven. My promised return. The quest-ion unmasked. Think of me when the clouds are burning. The oceans boiling. A Grail in the midnight sun. Unseen.

Ate the Serpent's heart. Learned
bird language. Called my darling
dear. Coo-coo-ca-coo. Never
coming home. Again. Simple. All
that serpent blood. A taste for
something new. Left Ireland for
Iceland for a tropical island. Grew
the sword from a rubber tree. Pulled
but Elaine held tight. The same old song.
In a magical stutter. Galahad was born.

The intensity of this game. Candlestick when it was open. Poetry does Not Matter. The game is played on paper. The pen is mightier.
Then wind. Hurricanes in the heartland. Signals from Korea. The game has moved to extra inning. Orange seats un-sat. The infield has moved out. The outfield has moved in. No explanation given. Real as a double play. Silent except for his radio.

Children should not sing. The Anthem is mightier. Static instead of words. The Flag is not there. Behold the empty sky. A dustbowl hovering. The wasteland's blown in. How quickly things change. Carry my heart in a bucket. The earth remains broken. Splinters in the perilous seat. All my loves and not a single returned.

Asked the magician for her hand. An older text. The confusion runs deep. Nu-go-eye-o? Who are you? The pen-dragon. Again. Nothing new on this earth. The same old song and dance. Notes from the deepest space. Traveling. Ain't got no home. A blooming cloud of dust. The Big Dipper. No horn of plenty. Chased round and round the Round Table. Her final broadcast. Repeating.

Didn't ask for much. The blood
of a child. No father. Pushed
baby Jesus into the Nile. Crawled
way down in a hole. Talked worm
language. Waited in your heartland.
Plotted my return. Needed a knight
more pure than green. Your little boy
fell in a well. I am the radio closing in.

Your once and future king. Confused. Wrong about the beginning. Once Upon A Time there was a sword. A hope when none would do. Look upon our heartland. The Grail noise. Silent. No blood in the veins. A father but not my father. The milkman returns. Unmasked. Bodies inside bodies. Sounds from the deepest space. Your once and future king. Lost but not forgotten.

Spring and a bundle of joy. Didn't see that coming. Slept in the Grail all day. No funny-bone. Just Rock-A-Bye-Baby. And he was gone. Why in his veins. California on his mind. Spoke in riddles. Crossed his heart and hoped to die. His jokes were not funny. Nobody laughed. Poor Galahad on Mars.

Heading North. Crossed a friend-
ship bridge. The Grail under my hat.
Protecting it from harm. A grave mis-
understanding. Loved the static like my
home. Way down in a hole. The regularly
scheduled program. Interrupted. And
then another. Only Grail music. All day.
Every day. Transmissions from the deepest
space. A station found but not my own.

Had The Grail but lost it. Closed
my eyes instead. Retired to the
Florida Coast. The Grail Castle was
no more. The dustbowl loomed. A life
without shelter. I used to be a Knight
of The Round Table. Perilous. Surprised
at how quickly things change. Predicted rain
on Opening Day. And it rained. Blamed the
radio for our loss. Notes from the deepest
space. Our Holy-Anthem continues to play.

Sat in the perilous seat. Served green eggs and ham. Not what I'd expected. A case of mistaken identity. Nothing new under the sun. Always did what I was told. Right foot on the black hole. Left hand on Elaine. The question remained. Un-answered. Jesus raised his hands. You know the score. Bodies inside bodies. Fingers on Orion's belt. After the magical stutter. Galahad was born.

Promised a kiss. Something
he could not gather. Followed
that Damn-ward frog. His head
was filled with marbles. Sin-
king. Heavy is the crown. Your
mission should you choose to accept.
Listened to Grail music. All day.
Every day. And then it stopped.
The last one standing. Not a
Perilous Seat remained. Empty.

Pulled a boy from my heartland.
And then another. These kids to
heal the land. Heal it how? A
simple question never asked. Do
you love her? Crossed my heart
and hoped to die. Knew he would
not answer. Even a broken record.
Turns. Surrounded by failure. Fated
to this table. A role I was born to play.

Rode into town. Rode out
of town. Not even sure what
we wanted. Grapes as big as
your fist. A joke of sorts. Said
if you ain't got the doe-ray-
me. And that was it. A rode-
block at the edge of the world.
Turn back turn back wherever
you are. And so I did. Right
foot where her left foot was.
The slowest journey home.

Grapes as big as your fist. Wheels go round and round. Needed a one-eyed jack. Hit me, I said. Hit me, she did. Found Lancelot instead. Replied that he was no-body. A lie if ever was told. Notice how harts constantly die. And then what? A tapestry un-made. Voices in the other room. Knock-knock. Who's there? A Magician under-ground. Waiting.

The Grail goes on forever. A light
beneath the closet door. Never
asked the question. Who is there?
Knocking. That is the way of The Grail.
An un-invited guest. Welcome to our
Christmas feast. This is my body. King
me, she said. King her, I did. Squinted
toward that damn-ward sun. The gravity
of your heart-land. Un-ending.

Wore fool's clothes under all
my armor. Visible as the moon.
But a cloud. That soft red gar-
ter. Setting. Sounds beyond
the drapes. A radio in his coff-
in. Speaking. If you ain't got
the doe ray me. Things I don't
understand. A Grail in my head
where none was before. Calling
me to supper. A father but not my
father. Asleep on the castle floor.

Shook The Tree. No knowledge came
tumbling down. A great gift of snakes.
Here today. Gone tomorrow. Naked
as the day I was born. And then
there was night. A dustbowl blown in.
Drank from that cold bitter cup. The quest-
ion remained. Un-answered. Voices
in the other room. Mirror Mirror th-
rough the wall. Green apples fall like rain.

Holding out for a hero. A tune played on my knees. Eenie meenie miny mo. Knew the cards were marked. A scapegoat for a scapegoat. Carried the weight of the world in a bucket. Up before dawn. Sang: come and get your slop. Pigs as far as the eye could see. The confusion ran deep. Awoke in the big apple. Raised my hand when the question was asked. A simple man for complex times. In a magical stutter. The dust-bowl was born.

Hung The Grail out to dry. Royal blood
turned yellow. My laundry never ends. Ask
and you shall receive. Nothing. An empty
stocking. All those clowns on Speedway. Flags
in the waning moon. Welcome to my heart-
land. An imposter for an imposter. This is my
body. Way down in a hole. Transmissions no
longer received. Pulled The Grail out of my hat.
And then another. A red balloon for you to keep.

No idea who my father was. Jailed for the lack. Gotta have a job. Sir Crazy. The walls began to talk and so I learned. A baby up to your thigh. Spoke about the priest and your mother. In a lake. Upside down. Those cards in your hand. I raise. You call. A suicide king in the hole. Mordred behind every corner. Counting treasure at the table. A bullet in his eye.

The promise of something better. Anything not tied down. Filled my pockets with your green green corn. Marched away from that damn-ward sun. A rebellion short lived. Jailed and forgotten. Didn't he die? A hurricane turns inside itself. Fool's clothes under all that armor. Let me see the mark death made Poor Lazarus. Alive in itself. Dancing.

Afraid I'll die before this gets done. Feel
the gravity closing in. Heavy is the crown.
A skull not fit to wear. The Green Knight
in a field of pumpkins. All those faces but not
my own. Galahad's head. Un-earthed. Carried it
every-where. No hard feelings. Played his part
to perfection. Found that heavenly gate. California
is the Garden of Eden. A black-hole at the edge
of the world. Your singular quest-ion. Consumes me.

Ate at the welcoming table. A spread
laid just for me. The loneliest meal ever.
No-body here. Just me and my lonesome.
Played chess against myself. The pieces
moving on their own. Imagine that. Packed
my bags and left. Moving into that damn-
ward sun. California is the Garden of Eden.
Saw Galahad on a ladder. Painting windows
for pennies. Kept the change in my eyes. A ticket
to Angel Island. No-body on this beautiful shore.

Noticed how things do not change. Kept
The Wasteland in my pocket. Turned it over
and over. Dust as far as the eye could see.
Felt the gravity in my chest. No-body left
inside his armor. I am the breadbasket off
this world. Echoes from the cheapest seats.
You know the score. Come out come out
wherever you are. A black-hole in the evening sky. Empty as the day I was born.

The dustbowl loomed. A book that could not be opened. The bastard son remembered a sword. This is my body. All those angry lambs. Crows go round and round. Ain't got no home. A barn beneath the sand. Here today. Gone tomorrow. Waiting for the storm to pass. A little boy fell in a well. I am the darkness closing in.

A song that does not end. Dead on
arrival. They keep coming. Knights
from the heart-land. Never had
a chance. Each and every one. The
promise of something more. Boys in
uniform. The brightest buttons you've
ever seen. Marching to the jail-house.
Now. A false hearted lover. Not even skin
and bone. The quest-ion. Impossible to ask.

Prayed with his eyes closed. Hated to see good food dis-appear. A curious problem. Here today. Gone tomorrow. A moveable feast. The Grail. Your heart. Potatoes at the end of the rainbow. No-body cares what you want. Seek and ye shall find. No-thing. A question without end. Come out come out whatever you are. A radio in his heart-land. Singing.

Grew sick of the radio. Commercials all day. Every day. Behold a world without end. The same old song. Construction in the sky and on a stone. A father but not my father. Hope when baseball would do. Tired of this continuous loop. Hounds and hens round the Round Table. Forgot my umbrella at home. Each inning called for rain.

Refused all help. The quest-ion was
for him alone. In one ear and out
the other. A soul loosed from its crown.
Never saw him again. Red armor stands
alone. Rusted beyond recognition. Not
even sure what he wanted. Just dis-
appeared. Here today. Gone tomorrow.
A fool at the Golden Gate. Laughing.

Treated like a little king. Made a home in the forest. A mother afraid of knights. Tired of bird language. The constant tug. Left good shelter for the city. Refused to change my clothes. Naked as the day I was born. Knew her by her apron. A flag overhead. This woman without end. Wrapped inside my armor.

Prayed for something else. A castle full of children. These knights are all the same. Their armor. Empty. Echoes from the deepest space. A table without end. No lightning but a knock. The dustbowl looms. Taking from each what each most needs. A Grail darkens my door. The end is close at hand. Remember the stain of Mary's face. Our best linen turned to dust. Welcome to Angel Island. No-body on her beautiful shore.

A ghostly hand inside my head. All
these thoughts but not my own. I am a
radio short and stout. Signals from the
deepest space. No idea how this began.
A case of mistaken identity. Drank from
that cold bitter cup. No-thing changed.
The heart-land remained. Broken. Dust
as far as the eye could see. A black-
hole in the center of my chest. Beating.

No longer looking for the Grail. Instead a simple question: Which side are you on? Ravens on a picket fence. One language I know too well. Wanted dead and alive. A funny place to be. Way down in a hole. Graffiti on my broken skiff. Fertile as the sky is not. These are the ruins you'll find. Fools' armor under all that stone. Alive in itself. Dancing.

The monastery was at hand. Moving counter-clockwise. No-body was happy. Backwards as the day was long. Never got to say good-bye. Roses in my rusty helm. The horses all gone to seed. Rescued her from what? The only question worth asking. Kisses sweet as wine. Of course the end had come. Ravens on a picket fence. Waiting for her call all day. The lawns were freshly mowed. A heart-land turned to dust.

Ain't got no home. Can't even fit into
these pants. Shirts of another man. You
tell me this is who I used to be. Welcome
back. This helm is no longer yours. Years
spent in the forest. Dragons on the out-field
fence. Fighting my way through trees. Naked
as the day I was born. Mad men don't wear
two shoes. Your breasts in the midnight sky.
Crying out for supper. A baby on my knee.

Two years in the forest. A quest gone horribly wrong. Drank from that cold bitter cup. No idea how this began. Mad as all hell. Mirror mirror through the wall. Crows on the outfield fence. Still as the night is long. Bodies inside bodies. This boy will change it all. Hurricanes from the heart-land. California is the Garden of Eden. Left them all behind. My baby in her arms.

Swaying though I've drunk no wine. Each journey begins with a single step. Believed these thoughts were my own. A radio in my head where none was before. Music only a Cylon could hear. Left me in her arms. A baby. Un-wanted. The most important knight who never was. Set out for the Grail. One foot before the other. A fool at the Pearly Gate. Laughing.

Tossed and turned inside his armor. Not a tornado but a fire. Our barn beneath the heart-land sand. I am the reason your towers lean. Heavy is the crown. All these things I'd rather not know. Mirror mirror through the wall. Foot-prints on her bed-room floor. A husband but not her husband. Loyalty when none would do. Signals from the deepest space. Calling me to supper. A song that has no end.

Like sands through the hour glass. A skeleton on the evening news. Your king and future king. Confused. There is no counter-clockwise. Here today. Gone tomorrow. The same old song. Mirror mirror through the wall. Teeth white as a picket-fence. The silence of your heartland. Footprints on her bedroom floor. Holding out for a hero. His quest-ion to heal us all.

No-body doubts that I am laughing. The Grail. Silent. Watching. This thing to heal us all. Funny. The way it moves from each to each. Galahad who never was. A seat where none have sat. Notice how Malory lived in jail. Damned if you do and damned if you don't. Just the way the cookie crumbles. Truths my mother knew. Always scabs to cross the line. One-body to house us all.

Drank until the well ran dry. Staggered out of that midnight sun. A Grail not fit to wear. Covered the walls with papier-mâché. And if her mouth will not open? The question was for him alone. In one ear and out the other. Hated to see good food disappear. Like sands through the hour-glass. This is the land your fathers bore. A moon not in the sky.

Tired of these Victorian Homes. Voices in the other room. Returned to the forest. Made green eggs and ham. Knew The Grail was watching. A quest-ion but not for me. Come out come-out whatever you are. Followed the ghost to Christmas past. Things my brother knew. I was once a knight of the Round Table. Ate until there was no-more. A fool in his armor. Waiting.

Knew exactly how this would end. A Sunday Roast that's not for me. Even the radio refused to play. These are the days of our lives. Taking from each what each most needs. I was once a knight of the Round Table. In one ear and out the other. Lost in a field of pumpkins. Naked as the day I was born. Followed the ghost to Christmas past. A candle in her eye.

Raised in a field of pumpkins. Your scarecrow without a brain. Filled with all you do not want. Waiting for the song to end. This is my body. A nest for you to keep. Eggs in the midnight sky. Mirror mirror through the wall. Shirts stuffed with other men. A hole in the side of my chest. Bleeding.

The Grail was there for all to see. Drank from that cold bitter cup. Her lips were red as cherry wine. A black-hole in the waning moon. Only one way this could end. Bulls on the outbound train. Ain't got no home in this world anymore. Neither cave nor castle. A station found but not my own.

Died into that cold bitter cup. A bridge that could not end. Turn back turn back wherever you are. Lost only what I'd lost before. Welcome to my heartland. A chest beneath the dustbowl sand. Leaking. This scarecrow to heal us all. In one ear and out the other. Your king and future king. Empty as the day I was born.

Found the table set with bitter eggs. Rode until they were no more. The Holy Grail fades away. This is my body. Her tongue has turned to dust. Once upon a time. Called everything stone. It was not so. Camelot was something else. A city in my lady's hand. Lick me, she said. Liquor, I did. Removed her glass slipper. A voice I'd heard before. This woman without end. Wrapped inside my armor.

Returned to the forest. Not a sigh but
a stutter. Blackbirds at my ear. Singing.
If you ain't got the doe ray me. A language
I know too well. Turn back turn back who-
ever you are. A question I could not answer.
The only knight who never was. Behold a man
without armor. Stumbling. There is no counter-
clockwise. These are the days of our lives. In one
ear and out the other. An echo which has no end.

other poems

AUTHOR'S NOTE
The poems in this section were written shortly before moving to Norwich and beginning *The Dustbowl*.

3. iv, 2008

That my cock
be described

As a bird
She says

I have a sparrow heart
resting on my breast

As a tree
She says

I have a sparrow heart
nesting in my chest

As a woman
She says

I have eaten your sparrow heart

4. iv, 2008

Green trailer in
the cherry tree

White blossoms
through the door

A tin roofed
John Deere day

A trusty Philips-
Head by night

There is mold
on the lampshade

and dirty socks
on the floor

I've begun to wait anxiously
for the mail at noon

Tax return tax return
where are you?

Drove a conduit pole
for a blue bird nest

Wore gray slippers
to the store

12. iv, 2008
Chasing Thomas Hardy

       You did not come
And sitting on the lawn, my feet went numb,—
Wet legs for loss of your wet blanket there
More than that found lacking in my nylons' make
That thigh high passion which can overbear
Reluctance for pure lovemaking sake
Grieved I, when, as the noon-hour stroked its sum,
       You did not come.

       You love not me,
And lust alone can't lend you loyalty;
—I know and knew unto the core
Oh human needs divine in all but name,
Was it not worth a little hour no more
To add yet this: Once you, a poet, came
To soothe a love-lorn fan; even though it be
       You love not me?

26. iv, 2008

Once upon a time
there was a Cardinal

And in the Cardinal,
an idiot.

The idiot could not
move. Koreans

Blame the ghost. Still
no light through the shades.

Say hello to the empty
bed. Paralysis is

The name of the tree.
Hello dear idiot

And I am hers. Deep
in flight the Cardinal

Could not wake.
And so fell through

Ghost and mirror
through shell and seed

to that place
in hand.

A tree could move
The idiot

and his bride
Could move. Awake.

30. iv, 2008
First out at third

Once upon a time

When the coach pointed
I fled.

Necklace briars
uncactus me

Believe it!

There is a man beneath
the thorn

René Descartes
Eeny meeny miny moe

The umpire has four eyes.

In the bottom of the 9th
I become a tree

and sprout beyond the bag.

I cry, "Matt Williams, climb on!"
And later I cry

When the groundscrew drags

The field and later when
A tarp is pulled over my head;

And the lights go out.
And the stadium is silent.

5. v, 2008 (Tucson)

Once upon a time

Power went out and
stars grew in fury

Linen hangs the surf;
a blanket is our only anchor

And that set sail so
here we float before land

Furrows in the loam of the moon

Soon there will be
breasts of all sizes

Thighs covered all too quickly

Good God Victorian Life;
wake me when this epoch ends

6. v, 2008 (Tucson)
Circa zero

Once upon a time

There was nothing.
There never was.

A tough place to start.

And then you were,
growing in the gloom

With paper stars;
a concrete moon.

I tucked into my socks

Yet somehow the night
strayed out of my shoes

and returned to the sky;
pierced by heavenly light

Depressions of lost bodies;
the nighttime in your thigh

14. v. 2008
Looking north in Tucson

Once upon a time
Houses were made of dirt
And dirt was bound by grass
And grass becoming mounds we sat
The beer was cold and I was
Cold and the graveyard
With its upright gravestones
And the upright dead each
On their back becoming dust
Swept into her skirt and so
She wore the skin of the dead
And I the ring of the soon to be

17. v, 2008
Lake Ticoa

The leaf to flower. The grass
is turning. The sky. No orange. No
dying red. No plane but birds. No
wind in still. The leaves. The buds.
The flowers. No plural. Each bird.
Each flower. Each gray trunk. Purple,
white. The lake. The shadow. The
trout below. Rainbow. Speckled.
Bream. Catfish. No fishermen
above. The sky. The bees.
The flowers. That one.
That wasp. Tucked wings.
Floats. Swallowed by the bank.

18. v, 2008
Blueprint

The house was empty. The doors
Were open. No dogs. No canned yams.
The floors. Gone. The walls. No walls.
The people. See above. Their skin.
Their bones. Their organs like hearts.
Donated. The recipients. Dead.
Neighbors. Moved. Animals.
Extinct. Film. Exposed.
Cameras. Pawned. No sink.
No roof. No frame. No pipes
To rust. No phone to answer.
No reason to close the doors.

21. v, 2008
Once in a blue moon
For Sang-yeon

The sky is dark in Seoul. No
Moon. No stars. No sun
For hands as small as yours.
No sun. No hands. These
Dreams. A wooden fence
Opposed to sleep. No night.
No moon. No eyes to see.

24. v, 2008
Brown Bag

Your eyes rain curfew.
No grass but dark will grow.
No days. No sun. No
Rose to sandwich. To say,
Our days are numbered
No days. No light. No
Fog to roll for change.

28. v, 2008
Rubble

In every picture. Doors.
Around every door. Debris.
Homes. Destroyed. Schools.
Condemned. No reason to
Duck and cover. Each student.
Dead. Each table. Collapsed. No
Tables. No children. Just doors.

1. vi, 2008
Bone

The sky is made of bone.
The moon. Bone. The
Stars. Bone. That cloud
Is floating bone. Blue-
Birds white as bone. Bone
Flowers. Bone bees. The
Willow twisted bone.

9. vii, 2008
Scene III

The windows. Gone. Just
Holes for wind. The sound of
Stars. The hallway groans.
So little remains. The door.
The chimney. Some tin for
Rain to play. No rain. No
Clouds but sky. A rising bird.
The vent of dust and flame.

11. vii, 2008
A late snow

The city. Black. The
People. Black. Their clothes.
The darkest black. Their
Teeth are black. Their
Eyes. No eyes so black.
Their hair is night so black. The
Grass they mow is black. Black
Wind that blows across the land
So black. Black snow that falls
On trees so black. On roof tops.
Black. Through chimneys. Black. On
Parasols that hold the sky so black.

18. vii, 2008
Of grass and night

Eerily. Wearily. The
Gray on even peach.
The color of bed is
Wait. The red in
Morning brings a
Chair to sleep. It
Snores the bug inside
Our screen. The light
In static stains her feet.
The smell of moon in full.